WILD HORSE SCIENTISTS

WILD HORSE
SCIENTISTS

Written by KAY FRYDENBORG

Houghton Mifflin • Houghton Mifflin Harcourt • Boston   New York   2012

To my family for their steadfast support, and for the animals who have enriched my life beyond words

Houghton Mifflin is an imprint of Houghton Mifflin Harcourt Publishing Company.

www.hmhbooks.com

The text of this book is set in Scala.

Library of Congress Cataloging-in-Publication Data is on file.

Manufactured in China
SCP 10 9 8 7 6 5 4 3 2 1
4500363326

Acknowledgments

This book was percolating in my mind for many years, but it would never have become a reality without Jay Kirkpatrick, Ron Keiper, and Allison Turner. I'm so grateful to all three for their endless patience and generosity in sharing a deep understanding of America's wild horses with me. I would also like to thank Lee Boyd, whose extensive knowledge and experience with wild horses in general and Przewalski's horse in particular were invaluable. I hope what I learned from her will find expression in a book yet to come. Thanks as well to Lisa Ludvico and David Powell; I asked and they answered without a moment's hesitation. I am also indebted to my amazing critique buddies: Stephen Aitken, Sheri Doyle, Karin Fisher-Golton, and especially to Judy Gamble, who helped make the key connection between the book I wanted to write and the perfect home for that book. All of them read multiple drafts and made crucial suggestions at every step of the way. You guys are the best. My talented photographers, Mike Francis and Amy Jacobs, went out of their way, sometimes on very short notice, to get the images this book demanded. My hat's off to you both. Thanks to the staffs of the Science and Conservation Center in Billings, Montana, and the National Park Service on Assateague Island for their cooperation. And finally, it has been my great good fortune in writing this book to work with not just one, but three extraordinary editors whose insights made all the difference. Thanks to Erica Zappy for her wisdom and boundless enthusiasm from the start, to the aptly named Ann Rider for picking up the reins with such skill in the home stretch, and to Cynthia Platt, who capably rode the rest of the way home.

Image Credits

Contents

Still wearing her shaggy winter coat in March, a wild Assateague Island horse blends into the twigs and grasses that make up much of her diet.

Stalking Wild Horses

IT'S A CLEAR SPRING MORNING, and Dr. Jay Kirkpatrick is back on Assateague Island National Seashore. It's the northern half of a barrier island straddling the border between Maryland and Virginia—a windswept, thirty-seven-mile-long sliver of sand, marsh grass, and piney forest. The island is uninhabited by humans but teeming with wildlife. To Jay, it's one of the most extraordinary places on earth. He comes almost every year—but not for vacation. It's the hunt for wild horses that brings him here.

Breathing in the sharp scent of the ocean, he allows himself a moment just to appreciate the natural beauty of this place, with its picture-postcard scenery so different from his Montana home. Just then a great blue heron steps from behind a pale green tuft of marsh grass. It skims gracefully along the mud flat on legs like stilts, extending its long

Assateague Island lies a few miles off the Atlantic coast resort town of Ocean City, Maryland. A sliver of shifting sand just thirty-seven miles long, it spans two states and contains more than 48,000 acres of natural beauty, home to many species of wild animals, birds, and plants.

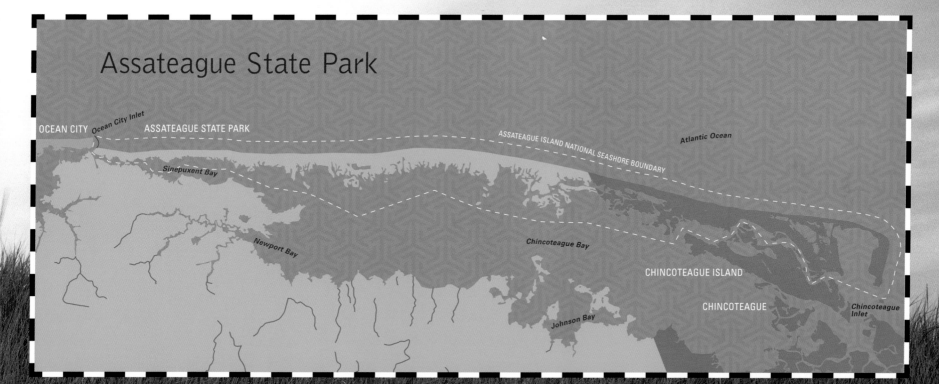

Assateague State Park

OCEAN CITY · Ocean City Inlet · ASSATEAGUE STATE PARK · Sinepuxent Bay · Newport Bay · ASSATEAGUE ISLAND NATIONAL SEASHORE BOUNDARY · Atlantic Ocean · Chincoteague Bay · Johnson Bay · CHINCOTEAGUE ISLAND · CHINCOTEAGUE · Chincoteague Inlet

neck and pointed beak with each slow, deliberate step. Jay watches until it disappears behind a gently waving curtain of grass.

Standing quietly beside him is Allison Turner, a biological technician with the National Park Service. Allison has worked for the NPS here for more than twenty years, monitoring wild species from endangered birds like the piping plover and bald eagle, to marine mammals and sea turtles, to the unwelcome mosquitoes and ticks that invade in summer. But the famous wild horses are her number-one priority. She keeps horses of her own at her nearby Delaware home, and she considers them her family. Working with the wild horses of Assateague is a perfect job for her.

She knows every one of them—their names and distinguishing marks, the makeup of their family groups (called

Assateague Island National Seashore, where more than one hundred wild horses roam free, is only a twenty-minute drive from the popular resort town of Ocean City, Maryland.

Assateague Island National Seashore

NATIONAL PARK SERVICE

Department of the Interior

NORTH BEACH ENTRANCE
United States Department Of The Interior
National Park Service

bands), their histories and their home ranges—better than some people know their own cousins. She watches their lives unfold through changing seasons and harsh conditions that her domestic horses, snug at home in their pasture and barn, have never known and likely could not survive. When Jay returns to Assateague each spring, it's Allison he depends on to help him locate the wild horses.

From the height of tall Atlantic seaside dunes, Jay Kirkpatrick and Allison Turner use binoculars to scan the surrounding area for wild horses.

Shifting his rifle to his left hand, he makes a sun visor of his right as he scans the horizon. Along one side, the marsh is bordered by tall loblolly pines that mark the dense interior of the island, where small horses can hide. They could be almost anywhere, playing and dozing and grooming one another, but mostly looking for food. They need to eat a lot every day, and they're not especially picky. Tall, flat blades of salt marsh cord grass, along with the spiky American beach grass that grows in clumps dotting the white sand dunes, make up the majority of their diet. They also eat thorny greenbrier stems, bayberry twigs, rose hips, various seaweeds, and even poison ivy. Occasionally they may dine on a bag of salty chips stolen from an unsuspecting tourist's stash. But most often they prefer the grasses. And they've definitely been here: Jay and Allison can see fresh hoof prints in the mud at their feet, where the grass is trampled. Moving single file along the indented trail, they head toward the scrubby forest.

An Assateague wild horse munches tall spikes of American beach grass.

A few minutes later Jay pauses to listen under a stand of pines surrounded by thick underbrush. He stares intently through some branches to his right. Then he sees her: a small, round-bellied chestnut mare. She looks especially scraggly with about half of her shaggy winter coat rubbed off from scratching on trees and sand. Her head is down, whiskery lips working overtime to separate out the tiniest edible leaves and twigs from the sandy soil at her feet. Her ears swivel this way and that.

Soon she'll be onto him, Jay knows. It seems the mares of Assateague get wilier every year. They can read human body language even from a distance.

Another diet staple for the horses is salt marsh cord grass, which is readily available but often requires horses to wade up to their knees for a meal.

Jay's convinced that they can recognize the National Park Service emblem on a uniform shirt, but even when he's tried wearing different clothes, like camouflage, they're rarely fooled. So instead of trying to sneak up on them, he usually starts a one-way conversation. Knowledge of horse psychology is as essential for this work as is a thorough understanding of biology and chemistry.

Jay and Allison have been tracking this mare and her band for several miles, following hoof tracks and manure piles. They've kept their distance, but now it's time to creep closer. If he gets within forty yards of the target, he almost can't miss. If

he does, there'll be no second chance—not today, anyway. It's lucky, he thinks, that he learned how to hunt and trap as a boy. He just never imagined, growing up in rural Pennsylvania, that those skills would come in handy in this particular way.

After a few more steps—quiet ones, with no sudden moves—he checks his target again. Allison freezes a few paces back. Even without using the range finder that dangles from a cord around his neck, Jay knows he's close enough now. Silently, in one fluid motion, he lifts the loaded rifle to his shoulder, takes aim, and squeezes the trigger.

A muffled *pop,* then a *whoosh* of compressed air. There's no deafening explosion, because this gun doesn't fire bullets; it's a lightweight .22, modified to

fire a small dart containing PZP at close range. PZP is the birth control vaccine for wild horses that Jay and his research partner developed after years of trial and error. PZP is what makes it possible for wild horses to continue living free on Assateague Island today, as they have for hundreds of years. Even after all the times he's done this, Jay still marvels at what he's just accomplished. This is it: science in action.

Working from the tailgate of Allison's National Park Service pickup truck, Jay and Allison often consult the master identification book to verify horses on their list.

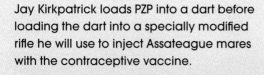

Jay Kirkpatrick loads PZP into a dart before loading the dart into a specially modified rifle he will use to inject Assateague mares with the contraceptive vaccine.

The Bureau of Land Management's Pryor Mountain Wild Horse Range is located on the south slope of East Pryor Mountain overlooking the Bighorn Basin of Wyoming, about seventy miles south of Billings, Montana.

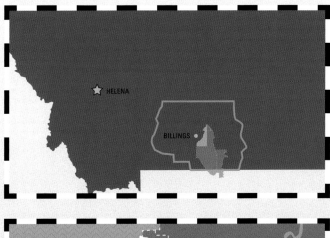

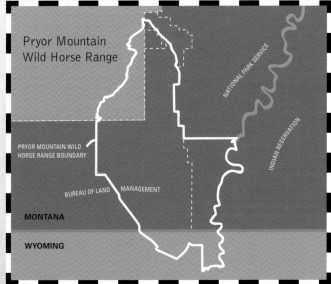

The mare's head flies up, more from the sound than from the sting of the needle. The dart pops back out almost immediately, as it's made to do. Unlike in the early days, the darts Jay and Allison use now almost always work properly. The wild horse trots off to the comfort of her band, no more concerned than if she'd been stung by a large, pesky horsefly.

Allison scribbles a quick note on the mare's page in The Book—a tool as indispensable for this work as the rifles and binoculars both scientists carry. The vaccinated horse's page is tagged with her individual ID—a combination of letters and numbers Allison can rattle off as easily as the names of her own horses.

Thanks to PZP, Jay and Allison feel confident that this mare won't give birth next year, and that will mean a lot less stress on her in the coming months, as warm days of summer slip away and a cold, wet Assateague winter takes hold. Before PZP, many Assateague mares died by the age of seven or eight, but now their average life span is longer than twenty years.

The first time Jay ever saw wild horses was very different from this day. It was in Montana, where he'd recently arrived to take a research and teaching position at Montana State University in Billings after completing his doctoral studies in wildlife reproductive physiology at Cornell University in upstate New York. His research interest at the time was the then cutting-edge science of mammalian embryo culture. Though he had earned his Ph.D. through Cornell's College of Veterinary Medicine, the study of embryo transplantation was of intense interest in human medicine as well. Eventually this experimental science would become routine procedure in human fertility clinics, enabling previously infertile couples to have children. But in Montana, Jay's research was about to take an unexpected turn.

One day in 1971, two cowboys had walked into Jay's office. They *looked* like cowboys—dusty hats, dusty boots and jeans—and they talked like cowboys too. But it turned out they were also biologists for the federal Bureau of Land Management (BLM), and it was now their job to manage wild mustangs living on the nearby Pryor Mountain Wild Horse Range. They'd come to ask Jay if he could find a way to make wild horses *stop* reproducing. Jay said he was sure that he could.

A band of wild mustangs gathers atop a ridge in the Pryor Mountain Wild Horse Range.

Little did he know then that it would take more than two decades to fulfill this promise!

Though wild horse population growth presented no immediate problem in 1971, it was just months after the U.S. Congress had passed the Wild Free-Roaming Horses and Burros Act, for the first time giving wild horses almost total protection from destruction by humans. Before, many wild horses on private and public lands had been rounded up and shipped to meatpackers, and the meat was either turned into dog food or shipped overseas, where it was considered a delicacy for human consumption.

The horse meat industry was unregulated and cruel. Terrified wild horses would be packed like sardines onto too-small trailers; many were severely injured or died en route to the slaughterhouses. The new law, dubbed the "Wild Horse Annie Act" after the Nevada citizen who'd worked tirelessly to persuade lawmakers to enact it, shut down the horse slaughter industry in the United States. It also mandated humane treatment for wild horses, long a special symbol of the rugged American West. But like many good ideas, the law would have unintended consequences.

The two BLM cowboys, says Jay, "knew that a train wreck was coming. The law gave absolute protection to a species that was incredibly fecund [had high rates of reproducing offspring] and no longer had natural predators. And there was no management provision in the bill."

It was this unintended consequence that started Jay on a lifelong quest to solve the wild horse reproduction problem.

The first thing he did was to enlist a research partner—his close friend and former graduate school classmate, Dr. John Turner. Together, says Jay, the two "set about to save America's wild horses." Jay was thirty-one. He believed in the power of science, and with their newly minted degrees he saw no reason why it wouldn't be possible for the two young men to solve the problem of excess reproduction in wild horse populations such as the one that roamed the Pryor Mountains.

They started by reviewing the available literature on wild horse biology and were shocked to discover that this consisted of only two unpublished papers. Wild horses had been almost entirely ignored by modern biologists until then.

They would have to start from scratch.

So Jay set out to find some wild horses to study. He'd headed out into the nearby mountains in his old jeep, following a path the BLM men had suggested might lead him to the horses. But finding them had involved playing a strenuous game of hide-and-seek in the wilderness, chasing after skittish and suspicious creatures who could run all day if necessary, or stand silent and motionless in a hidden canyon Jay didn't even know existed. He'd spent hours hiking up and down rugged hills of pine, stunted juniper, and mountain mahogany. Finally, when he was beginning to wonder if these wild horses were no more than a myth—something like Bigfoot, or the Loch Ness Monster—he discovered fresh hoof tracks and manure droppings. These, at last, were real—the calling cards of wild horses who had to be nearby.

When he spotted them, they were standing as still as statues, watching him intently from a grassy shelf on the mountain slope above. Then they began quivering and stomping, the herd stallion snorting loudly in his attempt to catch the scent of a possible predator.

They'd known he was coming; that much was clear. The multicolored band included a coal-black stallion and several mares—buckskin, steel gray, strawberry roan—as well as a sorrel foal painted with white socks and a snip on his nose. They were utterly unlike the domestic horses Jay had seen in the countryside near his boyhood home in Pennsylvania. These horses' wildness was apparent in the fiery, wary look in their eyes, in their trembling tenseness, in their rough, untended coats, and their readiness to flee. And flee they soon did, the stallion wheeling about toward the rear of his herd and whinnying explosively. He drove his band up the slope before him. Rocks clattered down as the horses raced up the ridge and disappeared in a cloud of dust into the maze of canyons above.

Jay stood breathless, watching them fly away.

For the next four years, he and John devoted themselves to observing wild horses in their natural habitat. They tromped across hills, gullies, forests, and sands; they slept out under the stars. Like the approximately 130 horses that roamed this unforgiving land of Red Desert canyons and high mountain meadows, they endured temperature extremes that ranged from 130 degrees Fahrenheit (54.44 C) in the summer to –40 degrees (–40 C) in winter. Jay and his wife, Kathie, still refer to this time as the "grain bin" years, because they often slept in a small government trailer that had been converted into a grain bin for domestic horses. At night, their sleeping bags would be covered with scurrying mice scavenging for bits of leftover grain.

It was during these years that Jay developed an abiding affection and respect for wild horses, which only deepened with time. He marveled at their grace and toughness. Life or death, for a wild horse, could depend on the precise path of a mountain blizzard or the lack of rain that turned precious water holes to dust. That was when he began to understand that "ideal numbers" of wild horse populations depended on many circumstances beyond any human's ability to forecast or control.

It was also then that he began learning what he needed to know about the physiology and behavior of these magnificent creatures. He started by studying hormone concentrations in the blood samples of wild horses. Accomplishing even this first step meant somehow obtaining syringes of blood from the very same wild, elusive mustangs Jay had barely managed to *locate* that first day. Luckily, BLM wranglers were able to safely capture and gently restrain some of the animals, so fearful of human touch, long enough that blood samples could be obtained. Those samples yielded the first clues to the reproductive biology of wild horses.

It was only the beginning.

Considering Color

The wild horses of America's barrier islands today come in many different colors and combinations of colors, and so do the mustangs of the Pryor Mountains and other wild horses in America. But the horses first domesticated by humans were all about the same color. That color was dun—a drab grayish brown or grayish yellow—with black manes and tails and black markings on their legs, and sometimes a black or dark brown strip running down the center of their spine. Evidence for this comes from ancient cave drawings depicting horses of that approximate shade. Now modern genetic science has given new proof of an ancient equine color explosion beginning around 5,500 years ago, and has suggested some reasons for it.

A 2008 study published in the journal *Science,* based on analyses of DNA differences among horse fossils, revealed that the great range of coat color variation in modern horses began soon after wild horses were first domesticated. This took place in the steppe region of what is today Russia, Kazakhstan, Ukraine, and Romania. The first new coat color to appear, according to studies of the genes that control color, was chestnut, a light, reddish shade of brown. Soon there were

Ancient cave drawings depicting horses have been found in many locations around the world. Perhaps the most famous are the drawings discovered in 1994 in Lascaux, in southwestern France.

also blacks and bays (dark brown with black mane and tail, and often black legs). Before long, these three basic coat colors were modified by other genes to produce "diluted" colors, such as palomino, and spotting patterns, such as pinto. Still other genes produced horses with white markings on legs and faces.

But why were ancient farmers so obsessed with the color of their horses that they began selectively breeding them this way? Scientists believe that the first horse breeders were selecting for tameness. But soon they realized that colored horses were more valuable in the eyes of their fellow humans for aesthetic reasons, too. Brightly colored horses brought greater prestige to their owners;

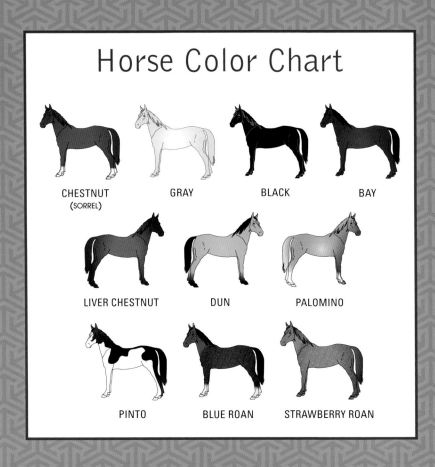

Horse Color Chart

CHESTNUT (SORREL)

GRAY

BLACK

BAY

LIVER CHESTNUT

DUN

PALOMINO

PINTO

BLUE ROAN

STRAWBERRY ROAN

Horses today come in a wide variety of colors and patterns.

The most commonly seen color pattern among Assateague wild horses today is pinto.

they were prized by kings, warriors, and explorers who changed the course of history on the backs of their colorful steeds.

Selective breeding for color didn't stop with ancient horse people. Three hundred years ago, most of the horses on Assateague Island were solid-colored bays, blacks, and chestnuts. Then, beginning early in the twentieth century, other breeds and colors were deliberately introduced. Today on Assateague you can still see solid-colored horses, but the predominant color scheme is pinto: a variety of flashy patterns defined by areas of white combining with bay, black, chestnut, buckskin (dun body with black mane and tail but no striping), or palomino.

In the Pryor Mountain mustangs of Montana, on the other hand, there are no pintos; the most common color is dun.

Dun color is created by a part of a gene (called an allele) that produces a lightening effect on the base color of the horse, and also adds primitive markings such as dark striping on legs or spine. Besides duns, there are bays, blacks, chestnuts and sorrels, palominos, buckskins, and roans among the Pryor horses.

Equine color genetics is a complex science. In the Assateague Island horses alone, at least seventeen distinct color variations have been identified so far.

A matching pair of duns living in the Pryor Mountain Range.

Going Wild

HORSES FIRST EVOLVED in North America over a wide area comprising what are now the Great Plains states. Scientists believe this because they can read the long record of fossil remains found throughout many parts of the continent and the world. The oldest known ancestor of the horse, *Hyracotherium* (sometimes called *Eohippus,* meaning "dawn horse"), was a small, rabbitlike creature that lived during the Eocene epoch, beginning about fifty-five million years ago. From that distant time, descendants of *Hyracotherium* continued to evolve in America until the modern horse—the genus *Equus*—emerged about two million years ago. Scientists who study fossil bones believe these early members of *Equus* would have resembled Przewalski's (shuh-VALL-ski) horse (*Equus ferus przewalskii*), an existing subspecies of wild horse closely related to our modern horse (*Equus ferus caballus*).

How did early horses travel from their birthplace in North America, across

FAST FACT

Przewalski's horse is sometimes called the only truly wild horse in today's world because it has never been domesticated, but by the late 1960s it had gone extinct in the wild. Luckily, the species was saved from permanent extinction through a successful international captive breeding program, and now Przewalski's horses once again roam free on the steppes of Mongolia, where they are called takhi. Their name means "spirit" in the land of their ancestors.

Fossil jaw of an eighteen-million-year-old horse (*Parahippus leonensis*) from the Miocene epoch, unearthed in Florida.

Three wild Przewalski's horses in profile.

miles and oceans, to Asia and Europe, where they eventually spread? The fossil record suggests they had actually migrated several times from North America, probably roaming back and forth across the Bering land bridge that once connected Alaska and Siberia before it disappeared beneath rising seas about 11,000 years ago. By then, horses had fanned out to parts of Asia and Europe and early man had spread from Asia and Africa to North America—probably along the very same route.

Fossils of horses that lived 15,000 years ago have been found in an area that is now New Mexico. But fossil evidence shows that suddenly, about 12,000 years ago, horses vanished from the continent. Why?

The Bering land bridge was a narrow strip of land about 1,000 miles (1,600 km) long that joined present-day Alaska and eastern Siberia at various times during the Pleistocene ice ages.

The reasons are still unclear, but an important clue may be that this was around the same time that humans first appeared in North America. Could early humans have hunted horses into extinction on the continent within only a few thousand years? No one knows for sure, but one thing is certain: had it not been for the lucky fact that horses had already migrated to other parts of the world, they would have become extinct forever.

Up until about 6,000 years ago, all the world's horses were wild, roaming across vast grasslands of Asia and Europe. Stone Age people still hunted them for their meat and kept some in captivity like cattle. Mares' milk provided an important source of protein and fat in the ancient human diet. But then, in about 4300 B.C., some brave and clever human tamed a wild horse for riding. Cave drawings found from that period in

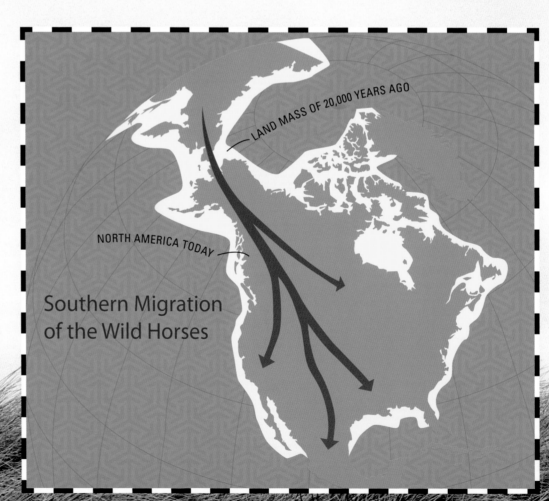

LAND MASS OF 20,000 YEARS AGO

NORTH AMERICA TODAY

Southern Migration of the Wild Horses

Ancient horses were a lot smaller than those we know today, as evidenced by this mounted skeleton of a full-grown *Parahippus leonensis* from the Miocene period in Florida.

Three-toed Transitional Horse

Ukraine show humans riding on horseback for the very first time. Equine jaw bones showing tooth wear from metal bits have been found, providing further evidence of domestication. From then forward, the relationship between human and horse—and the history of the world—would be forever changed.

Soon people in Europe and Asia began selectively breeding horses for their own particular uses: designer horses! This practice was especially successful in an area of Spain called Andalusia, and the result was the Andalusian—a medium-size horse with great speed, intelligence, and stamina, plus the ability to carry a

A small band of wild horses runs free on the beach on Assateague Island. These horses are descended from horses that were once domesticated.

24

heavy rider with all of his equipment. This was the horse first brought to North American shores by Spanish explorers near Vera Cruz, Mexico, in 1519.

After some 12,000 years, the horse was home again.

Soon more horse breeds found their way to America, often in surprising ways. As early as 1565, shipwrecked horses swam ashore to islands along America's Atlantic coast. And when England's king placed a tax on fences beginning in about 1670, settlers living in present-day Maryland and Virginia released their domestic horses on uninhabited Assateague Island to avoid both the tax and the expense of fencing their mainland properties.

With horses providing the means for Native American people to live nomadic lives where before they had been rooted in place, the animal became even more widespread and genetically diverse. And as horses spread across all parts of the continent, many reverted to a wild state after either escaping or being released by their human masters. By the 1700s, wild horses in North America numbered in the millions. In 1897, Nevada passed a law allowing any citizen to shoot a wild horse on sight. But with about two million wild horses grazing on public lands at the time, not many people worried about protecting them. There was not even agreement on how to *think* about wild horses.

Were they really wild, or were they feral—once tame animals that had escaped and returned to a wild state? Were they invasive intruders crowding out native wildlife, competing with domestic livestock, and trampling the grasslands?

More than a hundred years later, these questions are still hotly debated. But now most scientists believe that horses *are* a true native wildlife species in North America. They evolved here some four million years ago, whereas the earliest estimates of humans' arrival is a mere 50,000 years past. So from the standpoint of the horse, it's *people* who are the exotic species!

But maybe even more important is what modern science has revealed about wild horses in America. Fossil specimens, combined with sophisticated DNA analysis, have proven that today's so-called feral horses are the very same species as the last known prehistoric horse on the North American continent!

So despite their 12,000-year journey around the globe, American wild horses of today can claim a legitimate birthright to the lands they graze. They are ancient wanderers who somehow—against all odds—found their way home again.

So are wild horses really wild? If being wild means surviving in all kinds of environments with no help from human beings, the answer is yes. If it means that the domestic cousins of wild horses remain so close to their wild nature that those who escape or are abandoned by their human caretakers will quickly revert to a wild state, then there's no question that the answer is yes. If it means that generations of horses are born wild and live their entire lives without being touched by a human hand, then yes, wild horses still survive in America.

That's what happened with the horses of Assateague Island—survivors of shipwrecks or descendants of horses turned loose by mainlanders hoping to save some money. Now, nearly 350 years later, the horses of Assateague—often mistaken for cute, cuddly, tame ponies—are in many ways as wild as if their ancestors had never been tamed.

When Is a Pony Really a Horse? Sorting Out Sizes

THE TERMS PONY AND HORSE can get confusing. Is a pony a breed of horse, or simply a size? The answer: both! Most people consider a pony to be any horse less than 14.2 hands, but there are many exceptions to the rule. Traditional pony breeds such as the Shetland, Welsh, or Connemara are generally considered ponies even if they grow slightly larger than 14.2 hands, while some so-called horse breeds such as the Icelandic horse are quite often less than 14.2 hands but are still called horses. And the Falabella, a miniature horse breed, is rarely much taller than eight or nine hands.

Hyracotherium, the first horse, stood only about two hands tall—smaller than many dogs today. By the time of domestication, millions of years later, horses were much larger, but still on the small side by today's standards. They came in one basic color, shape, and size: dun, stocky, and about thirteen hands tall. After more than

five thousand years of domestication, horses had not only grown much larger but there was now a vast range of horse sizes. The tallest horse ever recorded so far was Sampson, a draft breed (used primarily for pulling and other heavy labor rather than riding) called a Shire, foaled in 1846 in England. By age four, Sampson had grown to over 21.2 hands tall (7 ft, 2.5 in/220 cm), and his owner renamed him Mammoth. The smallest known horse is a dwarf miniature horse named Thumbelina, born on May 1, 2001, in St. Louis, Missouri. Thumbelina stands a little taller than 4.2 hands (17 in/43 cm). But in 2010, the owners of a miniature horse named Einstein, who weighed just six pounds at birth, challenged Thumbelina's title as World's Smallest Horse, making the case for a separate title for the smallest non-dwarf horse.

Such tiny miniatures are called horses rather than ponies because of both breed

standards and phenotype—observable characteristics such as body conformation and temperament. For example, ponies often have thicker manes, tails, and coats than do horses. They generally have shorter legs, wider bodies, heavier bones, and shorter, thicker necks than horses', along with short heads and broad foreheads. They may have calmer temperaments, too, and an especially high level of equine intelligence. Both phenotype and genotype—the inherited genetic code of an animal that can be somewhat modified by environment—determine whether an individual member of *Equus caballus* will be considered a horse or a pony.

Phenotype, genotype, and tradition are all factors that explain why wild equines living on the Virginia side of Assateague Island are called Chincoteague ponies while those living on the Maryland side of the island—once part of the same herd—are called wild horses. All of them, on both sides of the border, are pony-size, and their ancestry is mixed. They resemble small horses more than ponies, but what they're called today depends on where they live. The terms reflect more than just size; they also show a different way of thinking about the two groups of wild horses that share an island.

This warmblood mare, taller than seventeen hands, and her pony friend, who is only about thirteen hands, are both members of the species *Equus caballus*.

A stallion trots across a dune covered in patches of American beach grass, constantly moving to keep his band of mares together and prevent other stallions from stealing them.

28

Watching Wild Horses

ON A WARM DAY in May 1976, Dr. Ronald Keiper stood in the middle of a salt marsh on the southern end of Assateague Island. He watched a multicolored band of about twenty wild horses—mares, foals, yearlings, and a black and white stallion with a distinctive pink nose. They paid little attention to the big man in his jeans and high green rubber boots; it was as if he were just a rather boring member of the herd. But Ron's attention was riveted on them. His job was figuring out how these horses lived on their own through all the seasons of the year and the cycles of their lives—their individual behaviors, their social structures, and how they interacted with their environment.

The salt marsh where he stood was a wide expanse of wet grasses and other low plants that wound around irregular fingers of salt water along the bay side of the island. The grasses were dotted here and there with small, raised hillocks where pine trees grew, providing a bit of shade. It was peaceful on the salt marsh if you didn't mind the occasional tick that could crawl up a sleeve without notice, or the clouds of mosquitoes that would soon appear for the season. It was one of the horses' favorite places to graze.

Ron noted how vigilantly the stallion kept watch over his band. In the year that he'd been observing the Assateague horses, he had come to think of this particular stallion, known by the name Voodoo, as an old friend. Voodoo *was* old for a wild stallion—at least twenty according to local lore—but he still controlled the largest harem on Assateague.

Just then, in the distance, another stallion appeared. He left his own small harem to charge straight at Voodoo's! The younger stallion galloped directly at one of the mares. Ron quickly stepped aside as the muscular bay horse rushed past. The stallion tried to turn Voodoo's mare toward his own band, but somehow she outmaneuvered him and hurried back to the safety of her band.

Then old Voodoo rushed up to confront the brown stallion. Ears pinned flat back against their heads, the two reared on their hind legs and slapped at each other with their front hooves, like boxers. Loud squeals pierced the air. But after less than five minutes, the brown stallion abruptly turned and raced back to his waiting mares. Voodoo chased him halfway there, teeth bared, then trotted triumphantly back to his own herd. Ron scribbled furiously on his clipboard as the bay stallion and his band receded into the distance.

A fight between two wild stallions seems to have little effect on the serenity of the salt marsh. Even a wading egret appears undisturbed.

In January, Ron returned to Assateague during an exceptionally difficult winter. The winds howled, a layer of icy snow covered most of the marshes, and freshwater ponds had frozen over. Bundled in layers of clothing that did little to ward off the bitter, damp cold, Ron hiked around the island, taking stock. He made an unwelcome discovery: several horses had died from the extreme conditions. He found Voodoo among them,

recognizable by the distinctive black and white pattern on what was left of the stallion's once flashy coat.

Ron collected Voodoo's long white skull to take back to Pennsylvania with him. He would keep it in his office with that of Rose, a favorite Assateague mare who had died previously. For the rest of his teaching career, he would use the two skulls side by side in his zoology classes to demonstrate for his students the

bones of the equine skull, the long, age-revealing teeth, and the anatomic skull differences between males and females. But later that day he would write a somber tribute to the dead stallion in a personal journal he kept:

I spent many hours in all seasons of the year in the company of this stallion and his herd. Never once did Voodoo act aggressively toward me, yet he kept a tight rein on his harem of mares. Mr. Voodoo, the black and white stallion with the reddish mane and pink nose, will be missed. Assateague will never be quite the same.

Part of a wild horse's skull, showing the jawbone and a full set of teeth, lies amid pinecones and branches on the pine forest floor. In time, the remains of wild horses become part of the land where they lived their lives.

Wild horses often die alone on Assateague. Sometimes their bodies are never found, but often their bones will be discovered some time after they've disappeared.

In the 1950s and early 1960s, most of the Maryland side of Assateague Island was being developed as a summer resort. Then in March 1962, a powerful storm swept over the island. Most of the vacation cottages that had already been built were wrecked, and many wild animals—including horses—were drowned. The storm was a stark reminder that the shifting sands of barrier islands are not good places for human settlements. But they *are* natural places for wildlife, and can provide opportunities for people to visit for short periods of time to enjoy the beaches, birds, and wild animals without risking permanent structures. Since 1943, the Virginia part of Assateague had been established as the Chincoteague National Wildlife Refuge. After the big storm of 1962, the Maryland side of the island was designated as a national park, and Assateague Island National Seashore was created.

Wild horses have lived on Assateague for longer than anyone here can remember, but in 1976, ten years before Jay Kirkpatrick would first come there, managers in charge of the federally protected habitat knew almost nothing about them. It had been eleven years since the island was designated a national seashore, placing the National Park Service in charge of more than 12,000 acres and all the creatures that lived within. Now the original horses were divided into two distinct herds, each living on either side of fences that marked the border between Maryland and Virginia. Their welfare was overseen by two different federal agencies and governed by sharply differing management strategies.

On the Virginia side, the herd of about 150 horses—the maximum number permitted under a grazing permit issued by the U.S. Division of Fish and Wild-

Saltwater cowboys from the Chincoteague Volunteer Fire Company drive a herd of "ponies" into the channel between Assateague Island and Chincoteague during the annual pony-penning event.

life—was still kept in check by means of an annual summer auction of most of each year's foals. This traditional event had been going on in some form for as long as horses had been on Assateague Island. It was an old-fashioned roundup by so-called saltwater cowboys, followed by a "pony swim," during which the gathered horses were driven across a narrow channel to nearby Chincoteague, Virginia, for an auction the following day. Most people meant the Virginia herd when they spoke of the wild horses of Assateague Island. Ever since the 1947 publication of Marguerite Henry's popular children's book *Misty of Chincoteague,* attendance at the festival had steadily increased.

On the Maryland side, a much smaller herd was managed as a true wildlife species. These horses lived quieter, more private lives with as little human intervention as possible. But for the ever-increasing numbers of visitors to the island, the distinction made little difference. Most only knew about Misty and the horses of Virginia.

Chincoteague ponies, visitors called them, but they were neither true ponies nor legal residents of Chincoteague.

Biologically speaking, these ponies were small horses, their size stunted by poor diet and stressful living conditions. And they lived on Assateague Island, not on the smaller resort island of Chincoteague that lay between Assateague and the mainland. The park rangers and wildlife specialists of Assateague knew these things, of course, but they knew little else about the horses. Though romantic legends and theories about them were plentiful, actual facts were scarce.

What did the horses eat, and where did they find fresh water? When and where did they give birth to their foals, and what happened to them in the winter?

These were just a few of the many questions visitors to the island asked; rangers and staff needed answers. They also needed to know things visitors might *not* ask but that would help them properly manage the fragile island ecosystem:

What was the impact of these large, grass-eating mammals on other animals, such as the native deer living here, and on endangered shore birds, beach grasses, and shifting dunes? How fast were wild horse numbers increasing?

Sika deer, one of two different types of deer found on Assateague Island, are a variety of small elk that is native to Japan. They were released on Assateague Island during the 1920s and today they compete with the native whitetail deer. Both seem to coexist peacefully with the wild horses whose habitat they share.

When the National Park Service went looking for a scientist to help them understand the horses they'd inherited when the national seashore was created, they wanted a researcher who would approach the wild horses from a purely scientific point of view. The perfect candidate would have no preconceived ideas about horses at all. Not only that, but this person would have to be willing to stay for several years, and to work in all seasons, despite heat, humidity, damp cold, high winds, and biting insects.

Hoof prints in the sand don't always lead in a straight line!

That person was Ron Keiper. He's an ethologist—a zoologist who studies the behavior of animals in their natural habitat. He'd grown up in a city and knew almost *nothing* about horses when he began studying the herds at Assateague during a six-month break from his job teaching biology at a Pennsylvania State University branch campus. Nor did he know then that this project would be the beginning of the most important experience of his professional life.

But he *does* remember clearly his first day on the job.

"I walked out into the salt marsh," Ron says, "saw a band of horses, and approached cautiously—sneaking up on them. I got closer and closer, and *still* they had not run away from me. Eventually, there was no more brush to hide in, just open space between me and the horses, so out I went, and . . . *no reaction!* That taught me that the horses were acclimated to people and that I could get 'up close and personal.'"

Does this mean the Assateague ponies were less "wild" than their Montana cousins? Ron doesn't think so.

"To me," he says, "*wild* does not mean the horses run away from humans when you approach them. To me, *wild* means that the horses do their own thing. They find their own food and water, birth their foals without human assistance, fight off injuries and disease. They go where they choose."

Science is about observing. Sometimes scientists observe life on a slide under a microscope. And sometimes they observe life in the middle of a salt marsh, standing in water up to their knees!

Over time, Ron found answers to most of the pressing questions about the wild horses of Assateague, and laid the groundwork for important scientific and management advances to follow, simply by watching.

But the *way* he watched was important.

First he had to figure out a system for identifying and tracking each individual horse on the island so he could map out social relationships, births, and deaths. Ron's system is still used by biologists on Assateague more than thirty years later. Each horse was photographed, and its specific color and markings were

Ron devised a system of identifying and recording the horses and their family bands that is still used on Assateague today. This is a page from one of Ron's original identification notebooks, showing a pinto horse from the band Ron assigned the letter B.

recorded by hand on an identification sheet showing left and right sides, front and back. The identification pages were kept in thick loose-leaf binders. Each horse band was assigned a letter, and each horse in the band a number. Foals were given the mother's designation, plus a letter indicating the year of birth (A for 1976, the first year the system was put into operation). Though N2B-E is not such a warm and fuzzy name, it does tell the researchers and rangers a lot about the horse and its relationships. Not every horse got a "pet" name in addition to the official designation, but many did: Comma, for the shape of a white flash on a chestnut face, or Nasty, for obvious reasons!

After identifying the different herds on the island and mapping out their home ranges, Ron would pick one band and go into the field to observe it. He made no attempt to approach the horses or change their behavior in any way, so that he could observe what their natural activities would be. Each minute during his observation period, he would look at all of the horses in the band and write down any changes in their activities. He would make these observations for each hour of daylight and for each month of the year. He even observed at night, because the horses kept doing things all night long.

Did he get bored, watching wild horses all day long? Did he wish he could pack up his record sheets and watch TV instead? No!

"It was a wonderful experience observing the horses," he says. "Usually just me, alone, way out on some isolated part of Assateague. It was so relaxing, just watching the horses doing their thing. Unlike psychologists who study animals and ask the question 'What can you do?' (or 'What can I make you do?'), ethologists simply ask the question 'What *do* you do? What is your natural behavior?' Once you know what they do, you try to determine why they are doing it. So I never asked anything of my horses other than to allow me to be with them and watch what they did. It was so peaceful out there, and the time just flew by."

Slowly but surely, Ron began to fill notebook after notebook with careful details about how the horses lived. He knew which mares were good mothers to their foals and which ones were

35

A young foal follows behind her mom beside a bayside marsh. Most foals are born in the spring or early summer.

These horses have been driven to the ocean's edge by biting flies. Before long, they may be standing in the surf.

neglectful. He soon understood how foals and young horses used certain facial expressions and mouthing behavior to show that they were submissive and not a threat to another, stronger horse. He figured out which months most of the mares gave birth to their foals, and what time of the year old horses most often died.

He observed how horses often acted like copycats: one would decide to scratch its back on a particular tree, and soon all of its herd-mates would do the same thing, one after the other! As an ethologist, Ron called this behavior social facilitation.

He saw how the horses dealt with hordes of biting insects. More than floods and ice, it was the insects that seemed to cause the most misery for both horses and humans on Assateague. During the times bugs were most bothersome, Ron would wear long-sleeved shirts and lots of insect spray; sometimes he added a hat draped with mosquito netting. But the horses had their own strategies. One was an activity Ron called circling, in which all the horses in a herd gathered in a circle with their heads toward the center. Then one by one, each horse would leave the circle and run around the outside, using the other horses' bodies and tails to brush off biting flies.

Another solution they devised was to run into the surf, often standing in water up to their bellies — but no higher, so the water wouldn't go over the heads of foals. Sometimes foals would even nurse from their mother while all the ponies stood knee-deep in salt water!

But the funniest way the horses would combat insects was by befriending a bird called the cattle egret. Cattle egrets often hopped around on the ground near the horses' hooves, picking insects attracted to the horses out of the grass. Sometimes the egrets rode on horseback, picking insect meals out of furry coats! One of Ron's studies showed that cattle egrets got more insects this way than they did without horses nearby.

This stallion (right) relies on a friendly cattle egret to help combat biting insects . . . while another stallion (above) has a whole flock of bird friends!

During the years Ron observed the natural behavior of wild horses on Assateague Island at night, he sometimes needed to use special equipment such as this night vision scope, mounted on a wooden rifle stock without a barrel for ease of holding. Now he jokingly calls it his "sniper scope."

her eyes, near the ground, was another pair of shining eyes. Her foal had been born in those five minutes! Ron called the foal Niacin, another name for the vitamin B-12.

Sometimes, when Ron was watching a band of horses in the dark, the whole group would suddenly rush off to some other location for reasons of their own, leaving Ron standing alone in the dark with his flashlight. But not that night.

Besides simply watching, Ron asked practical questions about the horses of Assateague in their environment. As one way to get answers, he built "exclusion cages" to scientifically measure the effect of horses grazing on the delicate marsh grasses and dunes. The cages would keep horses from grazing and trampling that small plot of land but allow other wildlife in. At the end of the growing season, after the grasses had gone to seed, he would dry and precisely measure the amount of vegetation in the areas the horses had grazed and compare the result to vegetation in an area where they had been kept out. Studies like these are still used on Assateague and other places where wild horses share a fragile habitat.

Watching horses at night was challenging, because no artificial lights shone on the island. But it was often surprising and rewarding. For example, at 2:30 a.m. one July night, Ron aimed a flashlight over B herd as the horses fed in the salt marsh. The light picked up the shining eyes of B-12, a pregnant mare. Five minutes later he shined the light in B-12's direction again. Below

Even though they live on an island surrounded by salt water, Assateague horses have access to fresh drinking water from numerous natural pools on the island. More than thirty years after beginning his studies on Assateague, Ron observes the descendants of those he came to know as they quench their thirst in one of their favorite watering holes.

Science in a Salt Marsh, Science on a Sandbar

Lisa aims a dart rifle at a wild horse on Assateague.

OVER THE YEARS, Assateague Island has provided an ideal field research lab for scientists in fields such as biology, zoology, and anthropology. Many have come to complete graduate doctoral programs in these fields, designing studies, spending hours on the beaches and in the marshes observing wild horses, and analyzing their findings after collecting data in much the same way Ron Keiper began doing in the 1970s.

Dr. Lisa Ludvico, now an anthropologist on the faculty of Duquesne University in Pittsburgh, Pennsylvania, spent parts of several years in the 1990s studying reproductive strategies of female wild horses. She wanted to understand how assumptions about *human* behavior might distort our vision of animals. In testing this hypothesis, Lisa called into question some of the terms commonly applied to wild horse populations, such as *harem*. The word is used for a human practice in some cultures in which one man lives with more than one wife. Lisa collected and analyzed DNA samples from the wild horses of Assateague to see whether this was also an accurate way to describe wild horse social structure. It seemed so, with one stallion most often maintaining a band of several mares. But Lisa's DNA analysis revealed a surprising fact: the stallions she observed with their "harem bands" were, on average, the biological parent of less than half of the foals in their band! Apparently "their" mares were visiting other stallions from time to time, and making their own choices regarding mates.

Dr. David Powell, now assistant curator of mammals at the Bronx Zoo in New York, carried out studies on Assateague Island during the summers of 1996–98. For his doctorate in zoology from the University of Maryland, he explored the social behavior and reproductive physiology of wild horses. He

Assateague Island
Stallion Home Ranges In Study Population

N6BG

T3I

N9BK

N6D

N4E

N9CH

N10G

M8

MD
VA

North

0   mile   5

Like Ron, Lisa picked out one horse band at a time and studied it for hours each day. This map shows the overlapping home ranges of stallion bands included in her study.

wanted to understand why previous studies had shown that the island's dominant mares were more likely than less dominant mares to produce a foal that survived to adulthood. Were male horses naturally attracted to dominant mares, or could it be that the mares competed among themselves for the opportunity to breed? David combined long hours of observing the horses' behavior with analysis of hormones contained in their urine and feces for clues, since stallions investigate both to determine identity and reproductive status of other horses.

The results: both of David's hypotheses were confirmed. Stallions did seem to be more interested in mating with dominant mares, and dominant mares were successful in breaking up many attempted matings between stallions and less dominant mares. More work would be needed to fully understand why, but David points out that from an evolutionary perspective, it makes sense for the most successful mares to produce more foals. It's also possible that stallions, often *not* the most dominant member of

This horse shows the instinctive horse behavior known as flehman. It's a way horses can analyze chemical properties of the urine or feces of other horses, to determine many things including sex and reproductive status of those other horses.

their band, find it convenient to associate themselves with dominant mares who are!

David also collaborated with geneticists at the National Zoo in Washington, D.C., to help the National Park Service (NPS) develop a management plan for the Assateague horses that took into account contraception, the breed ancestry of the horses, and the individual pedigree of each animal based on DNA analysis. The point was to figure out what the ideal number of horses would be in order to maintain a healthy herd that would have a minimal impact on the island's ecology. These studies helped the NPS and Jay Kirkpatrick plan the ongoing contraceptive program for the benefit of both the horses and the island.

Wild Horses: Shoot to Save

It had taken thirteen years, but by 1984, Jay Kirkpatrick and his research partner had seen some promising results in their quest to find a way of controlling wild horse population growth. In limited trials with captive pony stallions, and then wild stallions that had been rounded up in Idaho, a hormone preparation they'd injected had seemed to work, reducing fertility of the stallions. The next step would be larger, more extensive field trials—*if* they could find funding and wild horses to serve as test subjects.

An *ABC News* segment on those early studies had caught the attention of National Park Service management on Assateague Island. Their equine population had swelled since being designated a protected species when the National Seashore was established. What to do? NPS managers invited Jay to test his new contraceptive approach on the wild horses under their watch. As a smaller, more contained population than their counterparts on the western ranges, the Assateague horses would make perfect research subjects.

The initial plan was to inject wild stallions with the hormone preparation that had worked with the horses in Idaho. But there was a catch: those horses had been rounded up by BLM wranglers. Once the horses were restrained, the hormone could be given to them by hand. The NPS philosophy was different. Assateague horses were considered wildlife; handling them to administer medicines would move them many steps closer to being less wild. So the island stallions would be given their doses *remotely,* using a dart.

And then the assignment grew even more daunting: the NPS staff wanted a hormone-based contraceptive for wild mares in addition to one for stallions. This had never been tried.

It took until February of the following year—1986—to assemble the equipment and materials they needed and prepare for their first research trip to Assateague Island.

🐎 🐎 🐎

A pair of chestnuts with long, flaxen manes and shaggy coats peer through loblolly pine boughs. Year after year, sneaking up on the Assateague mares to administer the PZP vaccine becomes more of a challenge.

This horse is munching on bayberry branches and leaves, a staple in the diet of Assateague's wild horses.

The darts Jay and his research partner started with in 1986 were extremely touchy and difficult to load and use. Here's Jay completing one of the many steps required to load each dart in those days.

Winter on Assateague is cold and wet. The island is a confusing maze of brambles, dense shrub, and greenbrier thickets. The terrain is deep sand in places, swampy mud in others, with interlocking "guts" that crisscross the bay. But for the team, the real problem was the darts, which were cumbersome to use and often didn't work properly. Each dose of the hormone preparation had to be mixed in the field, shaken a hundred strokes, pressurized, and loaded into the dart with cold, stiff hands in an awkward, many-step process involving three separate syringes. Sometimes a dart failed to inject its medicine even when the shot landed perfectly on target—the fleshy rump of a wild horse.

Jay and his partner, John, found themselves cursing those darts on many occasions, and often Jay wondered if what they were doing could even properly be considered "science." Most of their time was spent endlessly trudging through dense shrub and greenbrier thickets, peering through binoculars, and staring down into mud or sand in search of used darts, stopping often to consult Ron Keiper's master notebook of identification sheets that was the key to telling one horse from another. Despite all that, they inoculated six mares and six stallions that winter.

In June they returned to the island, this time to record the makeup of the different bands—which mares were associating with which stallions during the breeding season. This would allow them to track mares they would assume had mated with treated stallions compared to mares with untreated stallions.

One thing they learned on the second trip was this: if conditions on Assateague could be uncomfortable in winter, they were downright intolerable in summer. Intense heat and humidity, poison ivy, the dense, prickly greenbrier, vast numbers of ticks, and some of the most impressive biting insects Jay had ever seen—thick clouds of mosquitoes and the amazing greenhead flies that could rip through your shirt before tearing into your flesh. It was no wonder so many of the horses bore ugly wounds on their legs, necks, and bodies, apart from the battle scars most of the stallions displayed; Jay and his partner were soon bleeding from fly bites too, despite heavy doses of insect repellant and layers of protective clothing.

In October, John returned to collect urine samples. He sent them off to Jay for testing. Hormones would be measured in the mares' urine to determine if they were pregnant or not. Now they would find out if all their hard work was going to pay off.

Dr. John Turner, Jay's research partner, is an endocrinologist on the faculty of the University of Toledo College of Medicine in Ohio. He also leads the research effort into longer-lasting forms of PZP. In this photo from the early days of the PZP research, he's bundled up against a chilly March day on Assateague.

A wild Assateague mare munches on phragmites, tall perennial grasses found in wetlands. They grow in reedy stalks that look like bamboo.

46

The results were a disaster. *All six* of the treated mares were pregnant—even though the normal pregnancy rate of wild mares with no contraceptive treatment at all is only about 50 percent! For the two scientists, these numbers were more than a disappointment. They were an embarrassment.

In July, they returned glumly to Assateague to confirm what they already knew: there were the six adorable new foals following along behind their hormone-treated mothers. Hormonal birth control for wild horses wasn't going to work. Worse: the previously untested hormone "contraceptive" they'd given to the mares had turned out to be a fertility *enhancer,* providing a near guarantee of pregnancy! Later they understood why: the hormone had changed the metabolism of injected mares, causing them all to ovulate—release eggs—immediately after receiving the shots. But understanding the reason didn't change the results.

The experiment had failed, dramatically, and the project would surely be doomed.

But then came another surprise: *Submit a new proposal,* said the NPS. *We want this to work.*

So Jay and his research partner scrapped the hormonal approach and started down an entirely different path. At the University of California–Davis, a researcher named Dr. Irwin Liu had been working with a molecule called porcine zona pellucida—PZP for short. It was made from a membrane that surrounds the eggs of pigs (a.k.a. porcines). Liu's studies had shown that a vaccine made from PZP when injected into a female horse (or any mammal other than a pig) could stimulate her immune system to make antibodies against her own eggs. The mare's eggs then became incapable of being fertilized and pregnancy was prevented. Dr. Liu had submitted a proposal to try it out on a herd of wild horses, but the BLM had turned him down without explanation.

"Irwin was sitting around with something that worked and no place to field-test it," as Jay remembers, "and we were sitting around with a place to field-test something and no practical method. It was a most logical marriage."

The scientists agreed to collaborate. Irwin Liu would provide the PZP vaccine, and Jay's team of two would manage to get that vaccine into mares on Assateague Island. The NPS offered another small research grant for two more years' work, and the quest began anew. Thirty mares would be inoculated with three shots each of PZP, all remotely by dart.

On February 29, 1988, Jay injected the first free-roaming horse—the first free-roaming mammal of *any* species—ever treated with PZP. He fired the dart from twenty yards across the brambly marsh he'd waded and scrambled through to find her. An easy shot, once he spotted her—a plain bay mare with a small white star on the left side of her forehead, calmly staring back at him from behind a strip of brush. Jay dubbed her Vacs-1. It was a momentous event, but at the time all he could think was *Only eighty-nine more shots to go!*

This plain bay mare was the first free-roaming wild animal ever to receive the PZP contraceptive vaccine. Jay darted her on February 29, 1988, and promptly dubbed her "Vacs-1." She lived a long life on Assateague Island, and produced no foals after that momentous day.

For the next two and a half months, he worked harder than he ever had in his life. The days were long—physically exhausting and mentally demanding—with great stretches of boredom punctuated by frequent episodes of frustration. Equipment glitches continued, and being cold and wet became a way of life.

Sometimes Jay wondered if what they were trying to do was crazy. He came close to quitting more than once. But he knew this would be the last chance to prove they could control wild horse populations in a practical and humane way. If he and John succeeded, it would be a huge breakthrough for both wild horse welfare and their own scientific careers. He had to make this work!

That April, eighteen of the twenty-six mares that the team had already vaccinated twice received their third booster shots in a final, two-week push. By now most had become wary of rifles and darts, and were much harder to find. As it turned out, not being able to locate and dart the final eight horses, while unintended, offered a chance to test whether a two-shot regimen would work as well as three.

As his plane took off from the small airport near Assateague that April morning in 1988, Jay knew that he'd given all he had to give.

Wet: No snug barn for this wild horse. She's used to weathering storms without human intervention.

In October, the two scientists returned to collect urine samples from the vaccinated mares to determine whether they had become pregnant or not during the spring/summer breeding season. Just as they needed to administer the contraceptive vaccine without actually handling the horses, they also had to determine whether the mares were pregnant or not without touching them or interfering with their free-roaming lives.

The urine collection process was composed of equal parts boredom and intrigue. Jay and John had to watch the mares closely, sometimes for hours, so they could be ready when one urinated, and that intense watching revealed the fascinating range of behaviors that Ron Keiper had begun describing more than a decade earlier.

It wasn't that the smell of horse urine was unpleasant; it smelled a lot like new-mown grass. But picking it up after it had been deposited in sand was devilishly hard. The technique they finally devised owed more to the playground than the science lab.

"We would shovel the wet sand," explains Jay now, "with a high-tech plastic picnic spoon into a high-tech gauze square. Then we would pull the corners of the gauze square up like a sock and place it in a high-tech plastic baggie, holding the neck of each tightly. Next we would start swinging the bag in a large circle, with our high-tech arms, and more or less hand-centrifuge about 1.0 cc of pure urine out of the sand in the gauze and into the bottom of the plastic bag. Finally we would decant the urine from the bag into a high-tech vial and put it on a high-tech cold pack for the rest of the day. Like with all the other challenges, we found a way."

It occurred to Jay that if pregnancy testing could be done with a *fecal* sample, collecting would be a lot easier. Such a test didn't exist, but while they were at it, the two scientists collected matching fecal samples to go with the urine. At the end of this trip, Jay flew home to Montana with a cardboard box filled with frozen horse manure as a carry-on. Airport security probably had a good story to tell friends and family that night.

"Every time the box went through the x-ray machine they would ask what it was, and I would tell them 'Wild horse feces,' and they would just stare at me."

It would be more than a year before he'd learn that fecal samples worked as well as urine for determining pregnancy in wild horses. As it turned out, the urine and fecal hormone analysis he developed,

Cold: A shaggy horse with icicles clinging to his face still manages to find a bit of beach grass during the Assateague winter.

which could track the entire reproductive cycle of wild mares, would eventually be applied to all studies involving wild mammal populations and would be as important a scientific contribution as the development of PZP contraception.

But that wasn't what mattered most that November of 1988. What mattered most was what the urine samples would reveal. Were the twenty-six PZP-treated mares on Assateague Island pregnant or not? Everything hinged on that.

Late on a Friday afternoon, alone in his lab at the college where he taught, Jay ran a special laboratory test called a radioimmunoassay on the twenty-six samples from treated mares, and another six from untreated mares. This highly sensitive test is used to measure tiny amounts of substances—in this case, specific hormones—that are present in the body of an animal or person. Jay looked at the tape as it ran off the machine, and then he ran the test again.

The results were as clear as could be. Of the six untreated mares, half were pregnant, as would be expected. And then, one by one, the results from the twenty-six treated mares came rolling off, and the story they told was stunning: twenty-six nonpregnant samples. Not a single PZP-treated mare had become pregnant! It had worked! And not only that, the two-shot regimen had worked as well as the three-shot regimen.

"I stood there," remembers Jay,

"staring at the tape. I was staring at my career, my life."

In July, Jay and John headed back to Assateague to count foals. The counting was easy, because there were no foals with the PZP-treated mares. Not a single one, just as the assays had shown months before. The quest was over.

That night they celebrated in the dark, sitting on a jetty on the north end of Assateague, looking out at the bright

Only a narrow channel separates the quiet northern tip of Assateague Island National Seashore from the busy resort town of Ocean City, Maryland. Wild horses go about their lives little bothered by the sights and sounds of carnival rides and tourist boats just offshore.

lights of Ocean City. They toasted the horses, themselves, and everyone who'd either scoffed at or encouraged them along the way.

It was a thrilling success—finally!—but it was only the beginning. Next Jay devised additional studies—including a comparison between reproductive rates in the wild horse population in Maryland, where use of PZP had now been introduced in a limited group of mares, and in Virginia, where numbers were controlled solely by the annual removal of most foals. In Virginia, he found, the pregnancy rate was close to 85 percent among adult females, compared to only 45 percent in *untreated* females in Maryland, where foals stayed with the herd. This proved that wild horses become *more fertile* when foals are taken away, a phenomenon known as compensatory reproduction.

The work got easier in some ways and harder in others. The troublesome darts were replaced with new, improved ones in 1992, making annual vaccinations much easier to carry out. Further studies documented the safety of PZP and showed that the contraception was reversible for several years after mares were vaccinated. Controlled management meant a few new foals were born, while older horses died.

It was hard to lose those horses. It was like losing a friend. And now some of the mares, once so trusting, had become suspicious of the darting process and were almost impossible to approach. The knowledge that treated mares were living longer, healthier lives only partly made up for the loss of trust on the part of younger ones.

By 1994, NPS management on Assateague Island declared the PZP program a success and announced plans to implement it for long-term management of the wild horse population. Their first goal was to stop population growth at 175 animals, which they estimated would be accomplished within two years.

But then, more trouble. By 2000, the NPS was worried that while growth of the herd had been stopped in its tracks, the overall herd size wasn't decreasing much. Maybe PZP wouldn't work after all! Maybe instead some horses would have to be taken off the island.

The answer lay in population details so carefully tracked and documented over the years that PZP had been used. Jay now understood that contraception is a *slow* way to reduce the wild horse population, because once mares stop having foals so often, they become healthier and live longer lives than before. This means overall numbers will decline more slowly

In their early years on Assateague, the researchers were often approached by curious young horses, though direct contact has always been discouraged by the NPS. This lonely orphan colt briefly befriended Jay after the youngster's mother died of equine encephalitis, a contagious disease that has swept through the horse bands in some years.

A boxful of spent PZP darts. Each dart must be retrieved and inspected after use to make sure it has delivered the full dose of the vaccine.

Occasionally it's the scientist who discovers remains of horses who have died on Assateague. This is disturbing and often sad, but records must still be kept. Once a horse's remains have been identified, as Jay is doing here, its card is moved from the active ID book to the "dead book."

than if horses were removed from the herd, but over time they will decline steadily.

By 2004 the herd had been reduced to about 140 horses, well on the way to the NPS "final" goal of 120. But now the rules were changed! After more study of damaging effects of wild horses on the environment of Assateague, and extensive analysis of how population levels would affect the horses' genetic health, the NPS set a *new* goal: no more than 80–100 wild horses.

From 28 horses in 1962, the herd had ballooned to more than 170 in 1996, but only twelve years later PZP had reduced that number to 120. Now Jay worried that his life's work would be thrown away. He hated the thought of equine families ripped apart and horses sent away from the only home they'd known.

But in March 2009 came word that the NPS had decided against removing any animals to meet the new population goal; they would be patient, knowing it could be accomplished with contraception alone.

In 2010 the equine census stood at 115—within sight of the goal. On his annual field trip to Assateague in March 2010, Jay, now seventy, looks back at a list of "his" original twenty-six mares and realizes that only two of them are still alive. They've grown old together, he and the horses.

He'll keep coming to this place for as long as he can. Though the work never gets any easier, he says, "There is more to do here, and more horses to take care of."

Near the end of a long day in the field, Jay's special rifle hangs heavy on his shoulder. After more than twenty-five seasons tracking wild horses, he admits that his feet are beginning to feel the wear and tear. This sandy trail is easier going than most places on the island where horses live, often just out of sight.

A winter trek through the piney woods of Assateague Island in search of wild mares. Jay is wearing his lucky yellow cap, which he always considered a vital piece of equipment.

FAQ on PZP

Q. What is PZP?

A. PZP stands for porcine zona pellucida. The zona pellucida is a membrane made up of proteins and carbohydrates that surrounds mammal eggs. Pigs are porcines, so PZP is a molecule derived from pig eggs. In mammals, the ZP acts as a barrier, permitting only sperm from the same species to enter an egg and fertilize it.

Q. How does PZP work?

A. When the PZP vaccine is injected into the muscle of a female horse, it stimulates her immune system to make antibodies to the vaccine. These antibodies also prevent fertilization of the mare's eggs by a stallion's sperm—tricking the mare's immune system into blocking fertilization. This means pregnancy can't take place.

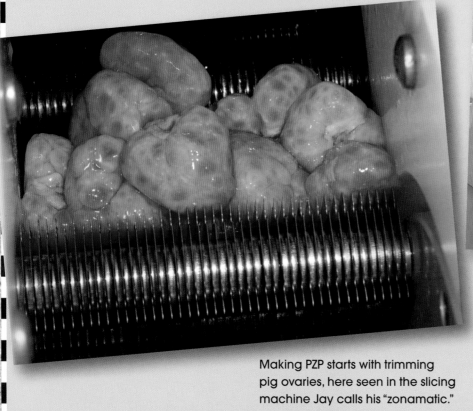

Making PZP starts with trimming pig ovaries, here seen in the slicing machine Jay calls his "zonamatic."

After slicing, the ovary material must be filtered. Here Robin Lyda, chief scientist at the Science and Conservation Center in Billings, Montana, is pouring the sliced ovaries and fluids through a series of filters to remove cellular debris in order to get pure PZP.

Q. Where is this PZP vaccine produced?

A. Most PZP currently used for wild horse contraception is produced by a three-person staff at the Science and Conservation Center, located in Billings, Montana. Dr. Jay Kirkpatrick is director of the Science and Conservation Center.

Q. Why pig ovaries?

A. Pig ovaries were chosen because a lot of research on them had already been done, because pigs have a large quantity of eggs in their ovaries, and because the pork industry makes available a ready supply of pig ovaries.

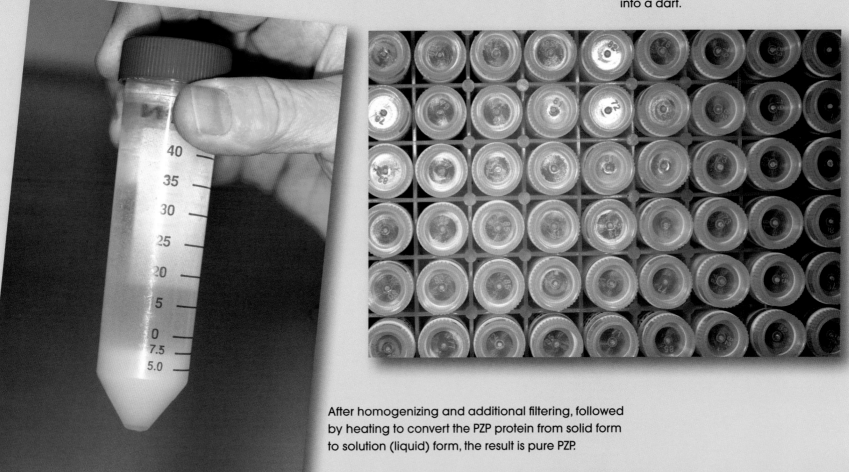

Once the vaccine is ready, each dose is stored in an individual container, ready to be loaded into a dart.

After homogenizing and additional filtering, followed by heating to convert the PZP protein from solid form to solution (liquid) form, the result is pure PZP.

This is what the PZP molecule looks like under a microscope, attaching itself to a mammal egg. The image is displayed on Jay's computer screen in his office at the Science and Conservation Center in Billings, Montana.

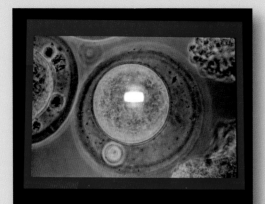

Q. Are pigs killed for the purpose of making PZP?

A. No pigs are killed expressly for their eggs; they are slaughtered for their meat, and no additional pigs are slaughtered for the purpose of PZP production.

One icy ball of horse manure, reading for testing.

Remote pregnancy testing is also done in the Science and Conservation Center lab. Here Robin is opening plastic bags of frozen horse poop mailed in the fall from Assateague Island by Allison Turner. Because the samples are frozen, any stink is purely imaginary!

Q. Is PZP safe for the horses? Can it harm the environment in any way?

A. In more than twenty years of use, no significant side effects have been observed in mares receiving PZP injections. The vaccine is 95 to 100 percent effective. PZP is quickly broken down in the digestive process of animals and poses no environmental hazard.

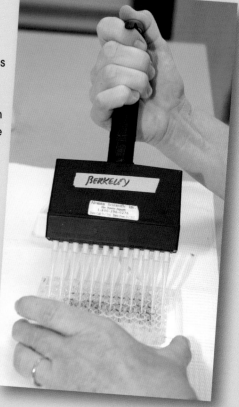

Testing hormones extracted from fecal samples to determine which mares, if any, are pregnant.

PZP does change the makeup of wild horse populations over time. For example, because mares are prevented from the stress of repeated pregnancies, they live much longer than before. And fewer foals born means that the average age of wild horses in managed herds gradually goes up. Overall, herds become healthier than they were before population control with PZP. Social structure of the harem bands may be modified slightly as a result of the lower birth rate, but this is still being evaluated.

Q. Is more research going on in the field of wild horse contraception?
A. Yes, several different approaches to wild mammal population control are currently being investigated. Dr. John Turner is directing the effort to develop a longer-acting PZP vaccine that requires only a single injection. The goal is to produce a single-dose vaccine that will last for three or four years.

Jay and his staff schedule regular target practice sessions, because accuracy is essential when darting wild horses with PZP. Ready, aim . . . fire.

High-fives all around! Robin, the Science and Conservation Center associate Kim Frank, and Jay congratulate one another on their shooting skills. Their target, a battered replica of a whitetail deer, is much more cooperative than wild mares ever are.

Three mustangs in the Pryor Mountain Wild Horse Range.

Forever Wild?

THREE MUSTANGS—a black and two duns—rest quietly amid juniper bushes, desert grasses, and wildflowers. Behind them rise the red-rock foothills of the Pryor Mountain Wild Horse Range in Montana. One of the horses reclines in the sun, while his two companions sleep standing up, ears flopped to the side. This is the same herd of wild horses that Jay Kirkpatrick first came to know in 1971, when the BLM cowboys asked him to find a way to keep wild horses from reproducing so successfully.

The horses were wary of humans then, but now they're accustomed to being watched and photographed. Thousands of people visit the refuge every year, many hoping to catch a glimpse of the pale palomino stallion Cloud. Cloud is an equine superstar, the subject of a popular documentary film and several sequels. His life has been chronicled since his 1995 birth on the range; now he's the most famous living wild horse in America.

In September 2009, the BLM announced a major roundup of the Pryor Mountain herd—one of many conducted by the agency for the purpose of reducing the numbers of wild horses on public lands in western states. Entire herds are driven to holding pens, individual band by band. Then some of the horses are removed for possible adoption. The rest are returned to the range.

Wild horse advocates have been protesting these BLM "gathers" for years, but this third roundup of Cloud's family, as advocates think of the band, galvanizes public opinion more than ever. A judge allows the gather to proceed despite public outcry over what many consider cruel and unnecessary intrusion by government into the freedom of America's wild horses.

A band of Pryor Mountain mustangs surrounds a photographer, paying him little notice—except for one curious young horse investigating the camera.

Cloud's band and the others on the Pryor Mountain Range are rounded up in the modern way, with the use of helicopters flying low to chase the galloping horses for miles into waiting pens. Hooves crash against metal corrals; stallions scream; young foals mill about, looking exhausted and bewildered. It's a chaotic and disturbing scene, and plenty of photographers and amateur filmmakers are on hand to document it.

Cowboys on horseback are aided by a low-flying helicopter in rounding up wild mustangs managed by the Bureau of Land Management.

Wild stallions battling while confined to a holding pen after a BLM roundup or "gather." Herding rival stallions and their mares into pens together can be very stressful for the horses.

Photos and video of the roundup begin appearing on the Internet almost before it's over. Within days, legislation is passed in the U.S. Senate directing the BLM to develop a new, comprehensive long-term plan for managing wild horse populations. Lawmakers cite complaints from the public that the BLM's current policies are inhumane, and they also acknowledge the reality that those long-standing policies are financially unsustainable for the agency, the country, and its taxpayers.

This young foal, identified by a number drawn on his back, waits in a chute while people gather around for a good look. He will be offered to the public for adoption.

61

Almost everyone has an opinion on the best way to preserve and protect wild horses in America. But the fact is that today there are only two ways to prevent their numbers from increasing beyond a sustainable level: gather, removal, and adoption, or fertility control. Reality will not allow for wide-scale reintroduction of predators on public lands, and allowing wild horses to suffer and die from starvation, thirst, and disease is not acceptable to anyone.

"There are no other choices in the real world," says Jay.

It's taken almost twenty years for Jay to fulfill his promise to the BLM cowboys; another twenty years have passed before the agency has tentatively embraced his solution to the problem of out-of-control wild horse populations in the West. But in January 2011, the BLM released a new five-year plan to manage the Pryor Mountain herd using PZP, in a program adapted from the one

A wild mare and her new foal make their way down a rocky slope in the Pryor Mountain Range.

62

Jay developed on Assateague Island. A similar plan will be put in place for all of the wild horses the agency manages. The BLM now says the use of PZP to control the wild horse population will greatly reduce or eliminate the need for large-scale helicopter roundups, which have been so stressful and disruptive to the horses and so costly to humans. For years, PZP has been successfully used to control numbers in small groups of horses in the West. But now, for the first time, the bureau is planning large-scale "catch, treat, and release" programs, by which wild horses are not removed from the range but simply treated with PZP and returned to freedom.

"That's progress," says Jay.

In 2010, about 1,500 wild mares in the West were treated with PZP, but now many more will be given the vaccine. The BLM says it will reduce the number of horses removed from the range by about one quarter, to 7,600 per year. With 38,000 wild horses and burros still roaming western public lands, and another 40,000, unadopted from previous roundups, kept in corrals and pastures, there's still a long way to go.

California horse trainer and riding instructor Karen Topping runs a youth program in which teams of kids and BLM-gathered mustangs are paired for one to two months of basic training and "gentling" to prepare the horses for adoption by the general public. Here, Kelly Mahoney works to gain the trust of a young mustang she's named Rambo.

Brooke O'Halloran, pictured here with Rambo, is part of Karen's youth program. She is helping Rambo adapt to a new life as someone's special horse. This is a happy ending for some of the wild mustangs removed from public lands, but there are still far more wild horses rounded up than there are people to adopt them.

Allison advises visitors in the parking lot about maintaining safe distances between people and fearless wild horses.

On Assateague Island, late winter is a quiet time for the wild horses. They still wear their shaggy winter coats, but the bitterest cold is past. The arrival of ticks, mosquitoes, and biting flies is still weeks away. The campgrounds are all but deserted, and almost no one walks the beach. The horses and other wild creatures have the island almost to themselves, unlike in summer.

Once the weather warms, a crush of visitors will mean Allison Turner spends a lot of time reminding them to keep themselves and their children a safe distance from the horses. She'll explain again and again that these horses are wild animals, even the ones who appear tame. They're unpredictable; they sometimes kick or bite, and every year a few people get hurt when they come too close.

For their part, some of the horses in the more developed areas of the island are so accustomed to humans that they've lost their natural fear. They're not a bit shy, and they can become dangerous pests—freeloaders looking for handouts. A few have been struck and killed by cars on the paved road close to the park entrance, where they wander without a care, stopping traffic and poking their heads into open car windows. They prefer grazing on the neatly mowed grass strips on either side of the causeway to remote, unmanicured marsh grasses. Sometimes they march up and down rows of parked cars near the state park and the campgrounds, foraging for potato chips, Twinkies, and Twizzlers. The sight of bright plastic rafts, boogie boards, and armies of small children does not in the least deter them from their quest.

Two chestnut horses make one of their regular visits to a parking lot as visitors arrive on a hot August day. The horses who spend time in the less remote parts of the island lose their natural fear of people and can appear to be tame even though they are not. These people are far too close to the horses for safety!

The horses continue on their rounds, patrolling the rows of parked cars in search of a tasty treat.

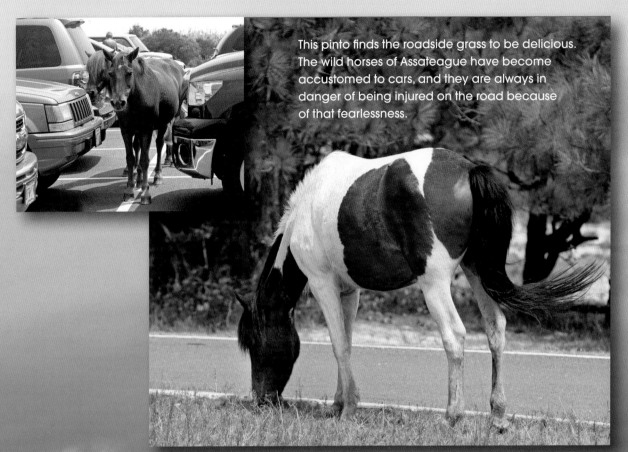

This pinto finds the roadside grass to be delicious. The wild horses of Assateague have become accustomed to cars, and they are always in danger of being injured on the road because of that fearlessness.

Early in the previous summer, Allison and other rangers removed a two-year-old stallion who'd grown up around the causeway and nearby state park area. Despite clear warnings from the rangers, visitors had petted and fed inappropriate treats to the adorable colt from the time he was born, and as he grew older he became aggressive. He began biting people in his search for food. Horses have sharp teeth and very strong jaws; their bites are no laughing matter.

"Finally we decided the stallion had to be moved before he seriously hurt someone," says Allison. "It was unfortunate, because it wasn't his fault that too many campers don't store their food properly, instead leaving a banquet spread out for the horses." Luckily, after a trailer ride to the southern end of Assateague, out of range of campers, the young horse quickly joined another bachelor stallion and seemed content to stay where he was.

A member of Assateague Island's Pony Patrol talks to visitors about the wild horses who graze calmly beside them. Pony Patrol members are trained volunteers whose job is to educate visitors about the animals, and to help both horses and humans stay safe.

After releasing the bird from nylon fishing line that had become wrapped tightly around one of its legs and offering it some water to drink, Allison frees the gull at the top of a dune, where it can catch a bit of summer breeze under its wings.

Allison holds an injured gull she discovered trapped in fishing line on the beach. She is responsible for many varieties of wildlife in addition to the wild horses.

For now, it's peaceful on Assateague. Allison has time to update the horse ID books begun by Ron Keiper more than thirty-five years ago, write necessary reports, and catch up on correspondence. Just as in Ron's day, visitors are full of questions about the wild horses, but now there are website inquiries and e-mails even when the visitors aren't here in person. It's time to take inventory and order supplies for this year's PZP darting too. Time for target practice with the darting rifle to make sure her aim remains as sharp as ever.

But most of her day is still spent in the field. Now it's mostly about the horses.

As she makes her rounds, Allison automatically performs a visual check of the different harem bands she sees. Some horses can look thin by this time in the year, but she's happy to find most of them furry and fat. The PZP-treated mares are in much better condition than they were before Jay's contraceptive program was begun, when they often gave birth to a new foal while still nursing its older sibling. Now each mare is allowed to have just one foal once she's fully mature, ensuring that her line will be represented in the gene pool. Jay calls it "an equal opportunity program."

At the end of February 2011, there were 112 wild horses living on Assateague Island National Seashore. This counts the sudden loss of N2BH, a twenty-eight-year-old bay mare found dead of a presumed accidental shooting during the two-day deer hunt allowed one January weekend. N2BH was a PZP-treated mare with twenty-three descendants, nineteen of them still living. So in wild horse terms, her life was abundantly successful. She was born on Assateague three years before Jay first came in 1986, and now she has died there. Injuries to horses are rare during the brief hunting seasons on the island, so her death was a sad surprise. Park service officials immediately launched an investigation and announced plans to prosecute the person found responsible.

Most horses on Assateague die from natural causes, not from stray bullets, and sometimes Allison finds their remains.

This striking bay colt with a Z mark on his hip is the only male foal born on Assateague in 2010.

And this is one of the two fillies born that year: Annie Laurie, a.k.a. N2BHS-I, born on June 28, 2010.

The current equine head count also includes three healthy foals born in the summer of 2010—two fillies and a colt. The colt is a striking bay and white pinto with a Z marking on his rump. There are a solid sorrel and another sorrel and white pinto born on June 28. The pinto filly, N2BH's granddaughter, is N2BHS-I, but now she's called Annie Laurie—named by the winner of an eBay auction held annually by the Assateague Island Alliance to help raise funds for ongoing support of the wild horses. Annie Laurie's mom is Carol's Girl (N2BHS), and her dad is Vinny (N6ELP). She has a lot of brothers and sisters—seven of them!

How can this be, with PZP? Allison explains that PZP works at least 95 percent of the time to prevent pregnancy in treated mares, but a few horses don't respond to the vaccine because of individual differences in their immune systems. Carol's Girl is one of those. But all seven of Annie Laurie's siblings are alive and well, so apparently the immune system quirk is just that, a quirk.

Because each mare on Assateague is allowed to have one foal before being placed on contraception for life, fecal testing for pregnancy is carried out on the untreated mares, so they can be given PZP before becoming pregnant a second time. In 2011, Allison was counting on just one foal from these untreated mares, and that baby would be born to N2BHS-B—Annie Laurie's older sister,

This is the other of the two 2010 fillies.

69

also known as Little Dipper. So the legacy of N2BH goes on.

Annie Laurie and her mother spend most of their time in the developed areas of the island where most visitors go, between the bayside campground and the state park. So the filly may spend her whole life in this same area and grow up unafraid of humans. But she will still be wild.

"What makes these horses special," says Allison, "is that they *are* free, living in natural social groups and showing the full range of wild horse behavior without interference by humans, except for

Two chestnuts on the beach at Assateague, mutually grooming in the age-old horse way.

And now, it's time for a nap!

This looks like a good place for a snooze.

population control." Though they may be descended from domestic horses, fending for themselves for hundreds of years in a difficult habitat has changed them. If you saw one standing next to a shiny, well-bred, and carefully groomed show pony, Allison points out, you might judge the wild horses of Assateague Island to be no more than scruffy little mixed-breed equines with lots of conformation faults.

But on Assateague Island, those "faults" are actually nature's adaptation that has allowed these special horses to thrive in their environment for more than three centuries. They live as they have for centuries, scattered over the island in quiet places most visitors will never see.

The only way Allison can get to them is on foot, sometimes after driving south past the paved road, along the wide sandy beach where the NPS four-wheel-drive pickup pitches and rolls like a ship tossed at sea.

Wild horses can be almost anywhere, but in late winter most will be grazing in the bayside marshes or resting somewhere in the loblolly pine forest. Their winter coats will blend into the vegetation, and they won't announce their location. Allison will have to hunt for them, but she knows where to look. The horses

71

she'll find in remote, often impossibly beautiful settings will ask nothing of her but to be left to their wild lives.

Like others of their species, these pony-size equines are tough. Wild horses have survived and thrived in almost every environment on earth, and have overcome everything humans and nature have thrown at them. What will the future hold for these magnificent animals? Will they continue their lives of freedom alongside humans and other creatures who share the same spaces on our planet?

With the dedication and persistence of wild horse scientists, along with their own resiliency, wild horses will survive.

How they will live, and where, is still an open question.

Allison watches from the shore as a band of wild horses takes to the bay at the sight of her dart rifle. Too late, though; she's already injected the last mare in line with PZP. Being a good shot is just part of her job.

Wild horses often form lasting bonds that provide the social fabric that protects and comforts them. Here a two-year-old greets her mother with a gentle nuzzle.

Glossary

anthropology   the scientific study of the origin, the behavior, and the physical, social, and cultural development of humans.

anthropomorphism   attribution of human characteristics or behavior to inanimate objects, animals, or natural phenomena.

antibody   a protein that is secreted into the blood in response to a bacterium, virus, or parasite and that neutralizes the effect of the invading organism or substance.

assay   qualitative or quantitative analysis of a substance, especially of an ore or drug, to determine its components.

bachelor stallion   a young male horse that has been forced out of the wild horse band into which it was born. Bachelor stallions will often join a group of other bachelors until they are able to attract one or more mares and start their own band. Also known as "satellite stallion."

barrier island   a long, relatively narrow island running parallel to the mainland, built up by the action of waves and currents and serving to protect the coast from erosion by surf and tidal currents.

chromosome   a threadlike linear strand of DNA and associated proteins in the nucleus of cells that carries the genes and functions in the transmission of hereditary information.

colt   a male horse who has not yet reached sexual maturity.

conformation   the arrangement of body parts of an animal in a more or less symmetrical way that approaches the "ideal" for that species.

contraceptive   a device, drug, or chemical that prevents fertilization and conception.

DNA   a nucleic acid that carries the genetic information in the cell and is capable of self-replication and synthesis of RNA, necessary for the transmission of genetic information.

ethologist   a specialist in the field of zoology who carries out scientific studies of animal behavior, especially as it occurs in a natural environment.

feral   having returned to an untamed state from domestication.

fertility   the condition, quality, or degree to which an animal or group of animals is able to reproduce.

filly   a female horse who has not yet reached sexual maturity.

foal   the young offspring of a horse or other equine, usually under a year old. As a verb, to give birth to a foal.

genotype   the genetic makeup, as distinguished from the physical appearance, of an organism or a group of organisms.

harem band   the natural social unit of wild horse populations, generally consisting of one stallion and one or more mares and their offspring. Sometimes one or more additional, or "satellite," stallions will also be members of a harem band.

home range   an area to which the activities of an animal or group of horses is confined, but which is not defended by the stallion of that group.

hormone   a substance produced by one tissue and conveyed by the bloodstream to another to affect physiological activity such as growth, metabolism, or reproduction.

hypothesis   a tentative explanation for an observation, phenomenon, or scientific problem that can be tested by further investigation.

immune system   the integrated body system of organs, tissues, cells, and cell products such as antibodies that differentiates self from nonself and neutralizes potentially pathogenic (harmful) organisms or substances.

infrared laser thermometer   an instrument that measures temperature using thermal radiation emitted by the object of measurement and guided by a laser for precise aiming.

inoculate   to introduce a serum, vaccine, or antigenic substance into the body of a person or animal, especially to produce or boost immunity to a specific disease or condition. Inoculations may also be called vaccinations.

invasive species   an exotic or alien species that causes problems in its new environment.

kinship behavior   the range of behaviors commonly shown by animals living together who are biologically related to one another.

mare   a fully mature female horse or other equine.

mustang   a small, hardy wild horse of the North American plains. Many are thought to have descended from horses brought to America by Spanish explorers.

ovary   the female reproductive organ that produces ova, or eggs, and in vertebrates also produces the hormones estrogen and progesterone.

phenotype   the observable physical or biochemical characteristics of an organism, as determined by both genetic makeup and environmental influences.

reproductive physiology   the biological study of the reproductive functions of living organisms and their parts.

salt marsh   low coastal grassland frequently overflowed by tide.

stallion   an adult male horse that has not been castrated.

steppe   a vast, semiarid grass-covered plain as found in southeast Europe, Siberia, and central North America.

wildlife reproductive physiologist   a biologist who studies the function of reproductive systems in wild animals.

yearling   a horse that is one year old or has not completed its second year.

zoologist   a specialist in the field of biology who studies animals.

Some Places to See Wild Horses in America

Assateague Island National Seashore
7206 National Seashore Lane
Berlin, MD 21811
(410) 641-1441

Chincoteague National Wildlife Refuge
8231 Beach Road
Chincoteague Island, VA 23336
(757) 336-6122

Wild Horses of Shackleford Banks
FSH, Inc.
306 Golden Farm Road
Beaufort, NC 28516
(252) 728-6308

Pryor Mountain Wild Horse Range
Bighorn Canyon National Recreation Area
    Visitor Center
20 Highway 14A East
Lovell, WY 82431
(307) 548-2251

If You Want to Help

DURING THE 1950s, an ordinary Nevada citizen—a rancher and secretary named Velma B. Johnston—became aware of the brutal manner in which wild horses were being rounded up on western rangelands and harvested for commercial purposes. She decided to do something about it. She spearheaded a grassroots campaign, involving mostly schoolchildren, who wrote letters to their legislators and local newspapers that brought the harsh facts to light. Public awareness, and the outrage that followed, ultimately led to the passage of the 1959 Wild Horse Annie Act and the 1971 Wild Free-Roaming Horses and Burros Act. Unfortunately, these laws were not able to eliminate all cruelty and abuse of wild horses in America. Recent changes to the laws passed by Congress have stripped some of the protections Wild Horse Annie helped make possible, and now thousands of horses are once again in danger of being slaughtered.

The good news is that there are once again bills in Congress that would prohibit the slaughter of any wild or domestic horse. On June 9, 2011, Senator Mary Landrieu (D-LA) and Senator Lindsey Graham (R-SC) reintroduced S. 1176, the American Horse Slaughter Prevention Act of 2011. When passed, it will end the slaughter of horses in America and will stop horses from being exported abroad for slaughter. One thing you can do to get involved is to read everything you can about this proposed legislation and write or e-mail your representatives to express your support.

But there are more things you can do to help. For example, you can raise awareness of the issue of horse slaughter and the pressures on wild horses in America by writing letters to the editors of your local newspapers and any equine publications you read. You can volunteer to help at a local horse rescue organization; some of the horses in their care may have been wild horses rounded up from the range, but all of them are in desperate need of care and support. If you witness an abused or abandoned horse, you can report this to your local animal control authority for further investigation. And finally, if you do own a horse that you can no longer keep, consider donating your horse to a rescue organization or retirement farm, or to a therapeutic riding program to help children and adults in need while also providing a proper home to the horse for life.

If you don't own a horse, you can still contribute to a horse welfare or rescue organization working to ensure protection and humane treatment for all horses, both domestic and wild. And if you or a family member is thinking of purchasing a horse, and if you have the necessary experience or knowledgeable help, consider adopting a wild horse or burro through the BLM's nationwide adoption program; information is available at the BLM website, along with more about volunteer opportunities in the wild horse program.

Resources

Books

Cruise, David, and Alison Griffiths. *Wild Horse Annie and the Last of the Mustangs: The Life of Velma Johnston*. New York: Scribner, 2010.

Halls, Kelly Milner, and Mark Hallett. *Wild Horses: Galloping Through Time*. Plain City, Ohio: Darby Creek, 2008.

Henry, Marguerite, and Robert Lougheed. *Mustang, Wild Spirit of the West*. New York: Aladdin, 1992.

Henry, Marguerite, and Wesley Dennis. *Misty of Chincoteague*. New York: Aladdin Paperbacks, 2006.

Keiper, Ronald R. *The Assateague Ponies*. Centerville, Md.: Tidewater, 1985.

Pomerantz, Rich. *Wild Horses of the Dunes*. Philadelphia: Courage, 2004.

Ryden, Hope. *America's Last Wild Horses: The Classic Study of the Mustangs — Their Pivotal Role in the History of the West, Their Return to the Wild, and the Ongoing Efforts to Preserve Them*. Guilford, Conn.: Lyons, 2005.

Urquhart, Bonnie S. *Hoofprints in the Sand: Wild Horses of the Atlantic Coast*. Lexington, Ky.: Eclipse, 2002.

Walker, Carol Jean. *Wild Hoofbeats: America's Vanishing Wild Horses*. Longmont, Colo.: Painted Hills, 2008.

Websites and Organizations

Assateague Island Alliance
www.assateaguewildhorses.org

National Park Service/Assateague Island National Seashore
www.nps.gov/asis/index.htm

U.S. Department of the Interior/Bureau of Land Management National Wild Horse and Burro Program
www.blm.gov/wo/st/en/prog/wild_horse_and_burro.html

U.S. Fish & Wildlife Service
Chincoteague National Wildlife Refuge
www.fws.gov/northeast/chinco

Pryor Mountain Wild Mustang Center
Lovell, Wyoming
www.pryormustangs.org

Science and Conservation Center
ZooMontana, Billings, Montana
www.zoomontana.org/science-and-conservation-center

Wild Horses: An American Romance
Nebraska ETV Network/South Dakota Public Television
www.netnebraska.org/extras/wildhorses/wildintro.html

American Museum of Natural History
The Horse: How Nature's Most Majestic Creature Has Shaped Our World
www.amnh.org/exhibitions/horse

Multimedia

Back to the Wild
National Park Service–produced documentary DVD featuring the wild horses of Assateague, available through the Assateague Island Alliance
shop.assateagueislandalliance.org/product.sc?productId=82

"Cloud: Wild Stallion of the Rockies"
PBS *Nature* series
www.pbs.org/wnet/nature/episodes/cloud-wild-stallion-of-the-rockies/video-full-episode/260

Selected References

"Domestication Led to Horse Color Explosion." Discovery Channel website. Accessed May 4, 2011.

Graslie, Serri. "Government Reins in Wild Horses Using Birth Control." NPR.org. January 6, 2011. www.npr.org/2011/01/06/132712168/government-reins-in-wild-horses-using-birth-control.

Kirkpatrick, Jay F., and Michael H. Francis. *Into the Wind: Wild Horses of North America*. Minocqua, Wisc.: NorthWord, 1994.

Kirkpatrick, Jay F., and Patricia Fazio. "The Surprising History of America's Wild Horses." *Natural History*. www.livescience.com/9589-surprising-history-america-wild-horses.html.

"Montana's Last Wild Mustangs." *Wild and Free Montana* (blog). January 25, 2011.

Pomerantz, Rich. *Wild Horses of the Dunes*. Philadelphia: Courage, 2004.

Robbins, Jim. "As Wild Horses Breed, a Voice for Contraception." NYTimes.com. April 20, 2009. www.nytimes.com/2009/04/21/science/21horse.html.

Index